Happy Talk

Happy Talk

Fun Ways to Talk to Yourself

by
Loretta LaRoche

Illustrated by Robin Ouellette

Lighthearted
Productions, Inc.
Plymouth, MA

Published by Lighthearted Productions, Inc.
15 Peter Road, Plymouth, MA 02360

For book trade ordering contact The Humor Potential, Inc.
15 Peter Road, Plymouth, MA 02360 tel. 1.800.998.2324
E-Mail: stressed@tiac.com

Printed by BookCrafters, Fredericksburg, VA

ISBN 0-9644014-9-5
Printed in the United States of America

Dedicated to
My Husband Bob,
who often says just the right thing!

Foreword

As a young girl, I lived near New York City. My mother loved the theatre and would often take me to see a Broadway play. I adored the music, the lyrics, the razzle-dazzle. Many of the plots and songs still lie just beneath the surface of my day to day reality.

One of my favorite plays was *South Pacific*. Early on in the play, one of the characters, Bloody Mary, sings a wonderful song called "Happy Talking" to two children;

"Happy Talking, talking, happy talk,
talk about things you like to do,
If you don't have a dream, you got
to have a dream, how you gonna make
your dreams come true?
Talk about the stars, talk about the moon...."

Rogers and Hammerstein

Long after the music stopped, the words remain forever etched in my memory bank. When we talk to ourselves and others about our hopes and dreams, our attention is focused on feeling good. When we realize we are in charge of our own happiness, we feel less like victims and more like victors.

Happy Talk was created with the thought that we can reduce some of our stress in life by reminding ourselves with little affirmations, that we can change how we feel by changing how we think.

Loretta La Roche

Chapter One

^{Not So} Fun Ways to Talk to Yourself

"If you expect the <u>worst</u> and get the worst
you suffer twice.
If you expect the <u>best</u> and get the worst,
you only suffer once."

anonymous

Not So Fun Ways to Talk to Yourself

I believe that all of us are born with the ability to be joyful, enthusiastic, positive individuals. One only has to watch a group of children playing, to witness high energy and tenacity. Conversations are liberally sprinkled with "my turn", and "I'll do it!", or "me first!". It has been noted that by the time we're three, we have heard over three hundred thousand no's! Our parents in their need to protect us, unfortunately also pass along some no's that begin to erode our ability to have fun, laugh, and think "Yes, I can!" To think positive becomes less and less an option as we continue to absorb the attitudes of those around us.... teachers, peers, even movie and TV idols.

We don't even know it's happening. But day after day, week after week, messages are being encoded in your mind. These thoughts become automatic. Eventually, you believe the conversations you have with yourself. Depending on your past experience, the self-talk can be loaded with self-doubt and act as a way of limiting life experiences. I'm sure we've all modeled negative self talk. How often have you heard people say, "I don't look good today", or "They might see me!", or "I know I'll say the wrong thing!"?

Many times I have mentioned to someone that it was a beautiful day, and instead of them simply agreeing, they seem to have the need to tell me when it's going to rain or snow, or when the next tornado is going to hit! There seems to be an internal voice that cannot bear joy for too long. I realize that there is sadness and suffering. However, let's not make it up when it's not happening. Let us begin to become aware of what we say to ourselves and others, and how it influences our lives. How we think can have a profound effect on our physical and emotional well being. It can help us all move to a more evolved spiritual consciousness.

Chapter Two

Words Can Wear You Out

"Ours is a world where people
don't know what they want and are
willing to go through hell to get it."

Donald R. Marquis

Words Can Wear You Out

Most of us realize that our emotions directly correspond to our beliefs and values and that they are the fuel that drives our behaviors. Although we may think we know what we want, we consistently feed ourselves (and others) information that gets us exactly what we <u>don't want</u> ... Does this sound like a Seinfeld routine? Well, in some ways our lives very much resemble a sit-com. Only we're not having as much fun as we should.

The conversations we have with ourselves and others direct our behaviors and actions. We can literally program our minds to seek out the negative or the positive.

Take a moment to reflect on how you greet the day, describe yourself, your job, co-workers, family, traffic or anything else that pertains to life on this planet.

You may have said the following:

I'm always tired

I'm never done

I can never lose weight

I always get the slow line

My family drives me crazy

I can't wait 'til Friday

Each statement leaves our body/mind with a "no win" message. The language contains permanence, as though it will never end, and leaves us with little hope, something the human spirit needs to survive. When we feel helpless and hopeless, it affects our immune system, leaving us vulnerable to a host of illnesses.

Is there life after negative self-talk? Indeed there is. Begin to integrate affirmations that can reprogram how you think. Does this mean you have to become a Pollyanna? No, it does not, since Pollyannas are ineffective and passive. However, it could mean that you could become more optimistic, cheerful, even happier.

The following chapter explains how you can write your own affirmations and contains a collection of over one hundred affirmations that are a combination of fun, compassion, hope, and success. Copy one or two down and repeat them to yourself throughout the day. The more you repeat them, the more they will become entrenched in your belief system. Remember, negative feelings took years to take hold and repeating this "Happy Talk" will help replace those that are less desirable.

Chapter Three

Fun Ways to Talk to Yourself

"Attitude is everything. Mae West lived into her eighties believing she was twenty, and it never occurred to her that her arithmetic was lousy."

Soundings magazine

The Eight Steps to Effective Affirmations

1. Make your affirmations short, clear and specific.
2. Phrase them in the present tense. You want them to start taking effect today.
3. Put them in very positive terms. Avoid words based on wish fulfillment, fear or negativity.
4. Don't make affirmations about changing other people. Direct the attention towards changing yourself.

5. Write your affirmations when you're in a receptive state. Perhaps after meditating or taking a nice long walk.
6. Keep your affirmations in handy places. Take them with you. Repeat them often. Keep in mind how long it took to create negative thoughts.
7. Change or rewrite your affirmations as you see fit. You may change your mind about a specific goal or need.
8. Have fun with them. Don't make them a job.

Words To Live By

Following are words that feel hopeful, loving, joyful and spiritual. Use them and others like them to create your Happy Talk.

Abundance	Adventure	Balance
Birth	Brotherhood	Clarity
Compassion	Communication	Courage
Creativity	Delight	Discovery
Dessert	Divine	Education
Efficiency	Enthusiasm	Excellence
Faith	Flexibility	Freedom
Forgiveness	Grace	Gratitude
Gusto	Guffaws	Harmony

Humor	Healing	Honesty
Integrity	Inspiration	Joy
Jest	Light	Love
Moment	Mirth	Openness
Peace	Play	Power
Prayer	Purpose	Release
Responsibility	Spontaneity	Strength
Simplicity	Spirituality	Surrender
Tenderness	Transformation	Truth
Willingness	Understanding	Wisdom
Zest		

2.
I enjoy being me.

3.
I am my own entertainment center.

4.

As long as I show up,
I'll have fun.

5.
I do not "should"
on myself or others.

6.
I allow others
to be themselves.
Otherwise, they'd
be phonies.

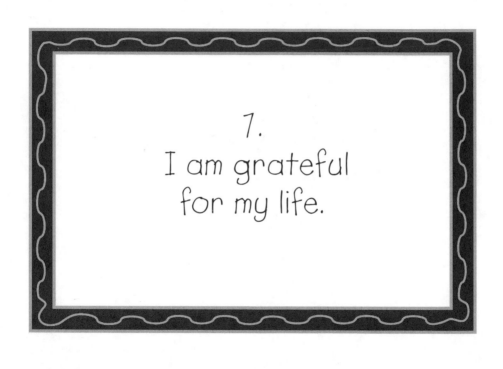

7.
I am grateful
for my life.

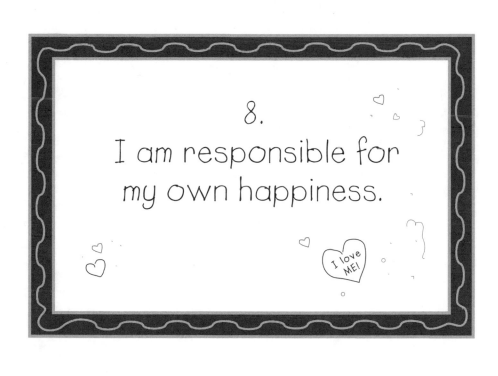

8.

I am responsible for
my own happiness.

I love ME!

9.
I learn from failure.

10.
Food keeps me well.

11.
I am a
moving experience.

12.
I observe rather
than obsess.

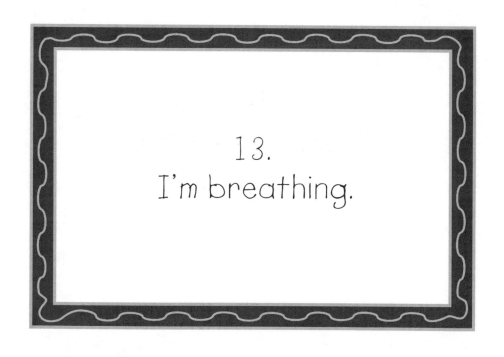

13.
I'm breathing.

14.
Others do not have
to change themselves
for me to be happy.

15.
I have stopped
hanging on
to regrets.

16.
I look forward to
new experiences.

17.
I laugh with my
heart and soul.

18.
My body
expresses itself
with joy!

19.
I am in tune
with nature.

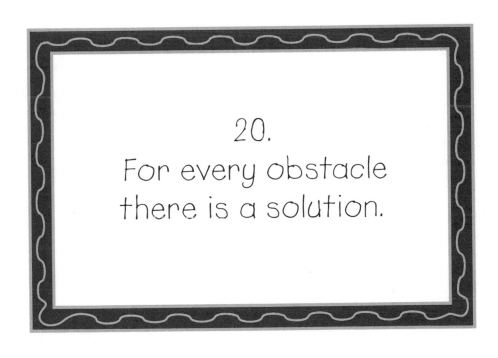

20.
For every obstacle
there is a solution.

21.
I appreciate whatever
is done for me.

Thank You

22.
I see the
humor in myself.

23.
I am free to
express myself.

24.
I play along
the way.

25.
I enjoy myself
and others.

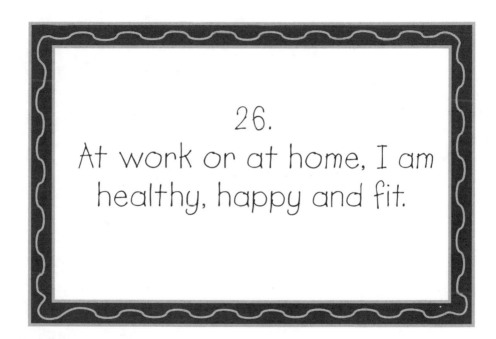

26.
At work or at home, I am healthy, happy and fit.

27.
I renew myself daily.

28.
I support myself with
kind, loving individuals.

29.
I "belly laugh" daily
and often.

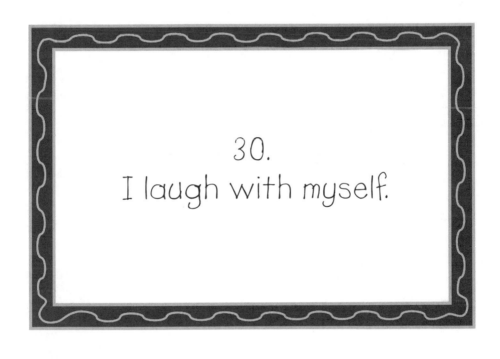

30.
I laugh with myself.

31.
I deserve pleasure.

MMmmmm.....

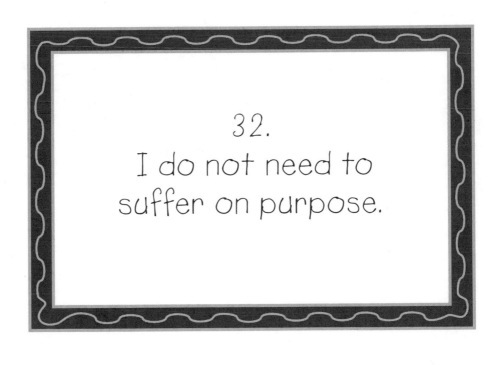

32.
I do not need to
suffer on purpose.

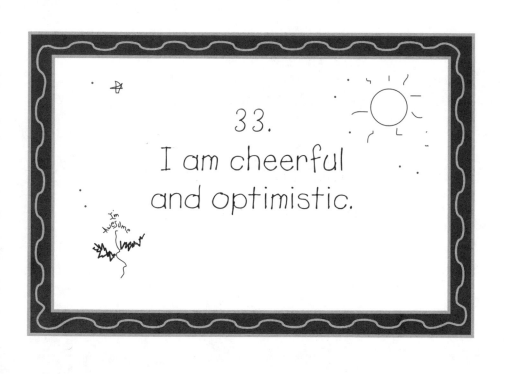

33.
I am cheerful
and optimistic.

34.
Hostility harms me.

36.
I accept myself.

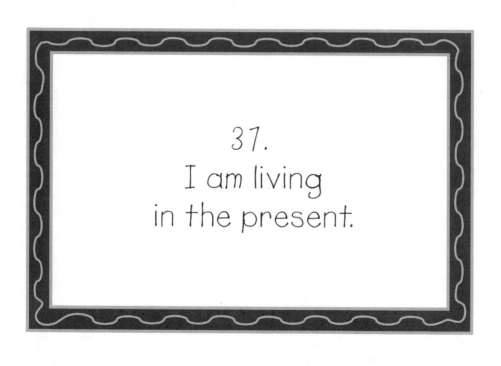

37.
I am living
in the present.

38.
I am patient
and kind.

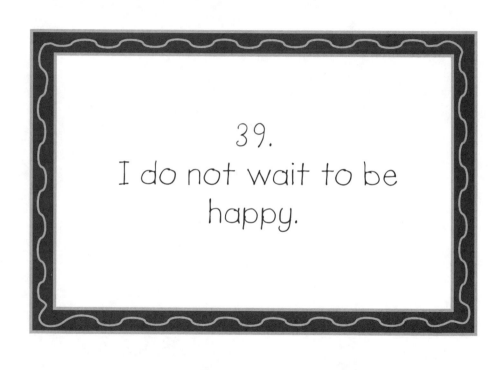

39.
I do not wait to be happy.

40.
Possibilities make
things possible.

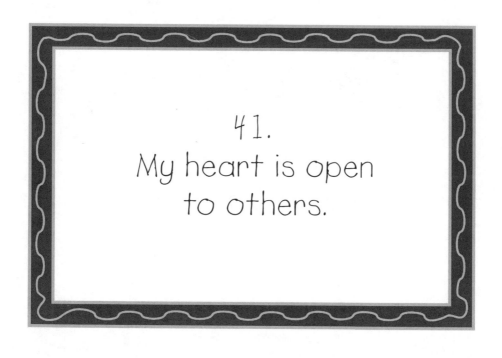

41.
My heart is open
to others.

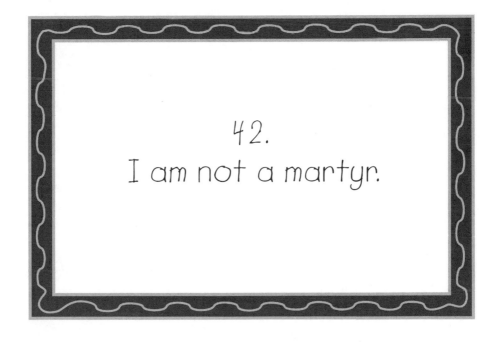

42.
I am not a martyr.

43.
I practice
being silly.

44.
I am growing older,
younger.

45.
I work well
with others.

46.
My work is
a work in progress.

47.
I risk living life.

48.
Deadlines
don't kill me.

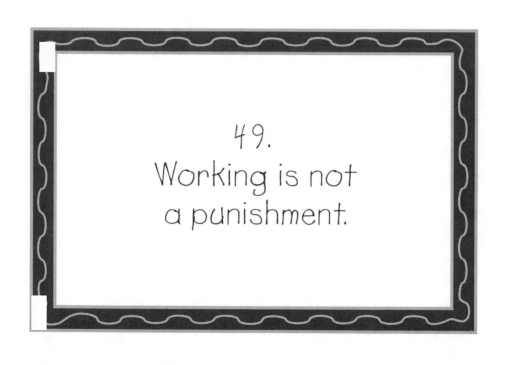

49.
Working is not
a punishment.

50.
Monday is just as good
as Friday.

51.
I listen just as much
as I talk.

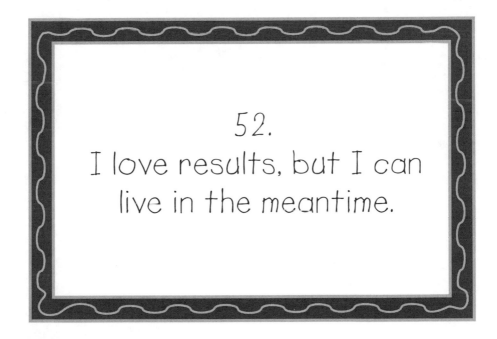

52.
I love results, but I can
live in the meantime.

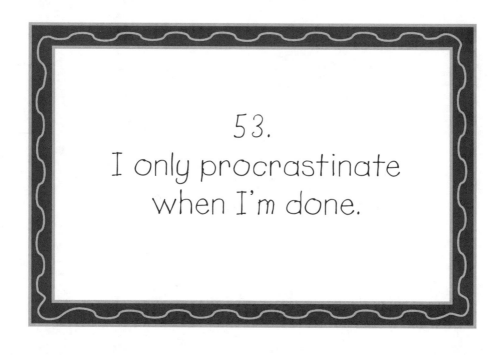

53.
I only procrastinate
when I'm done.

54.
I don't confuse "doing"
with "being".

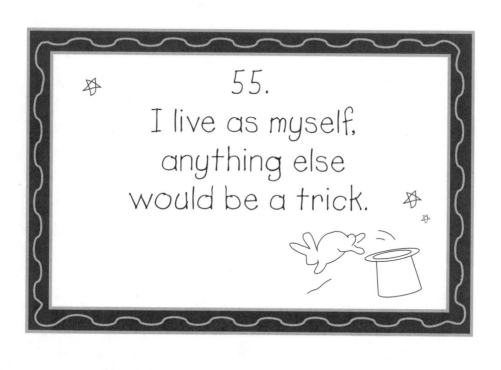

55.
I live as myself,
anything else
would be a trick.

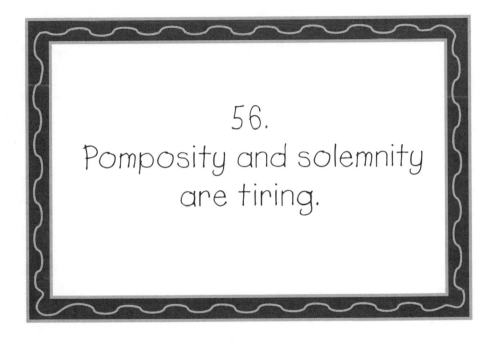

56.
Pomposity and solemnity
are tiring.

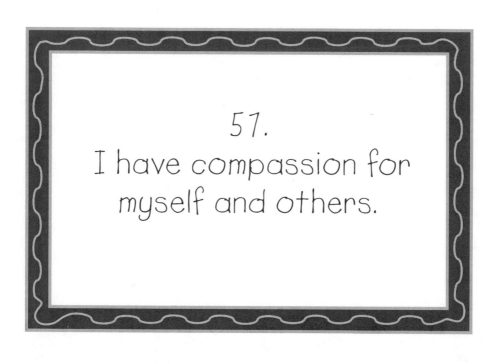

57.
I have compassion for
myself and others.

58.
I do not whine.

59.
Being challenged
excites me.

60.
I no longer blame.

61.
I enjoy being
alone with myself.

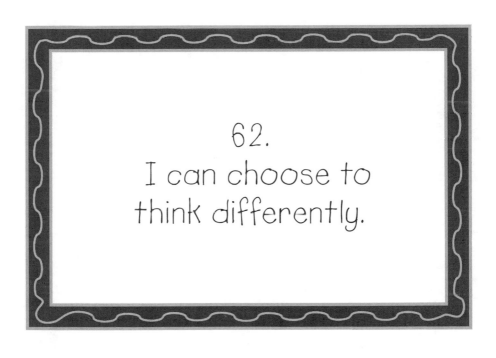

62.
I can choose to
think differently.

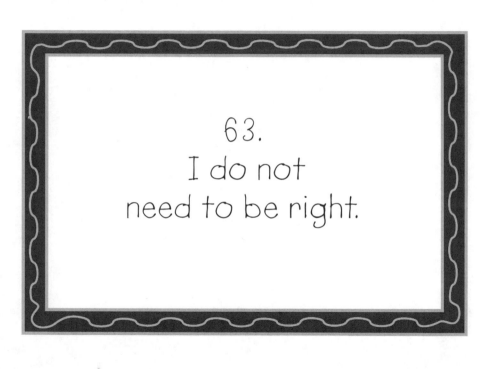

63.
I do not
need to be right.

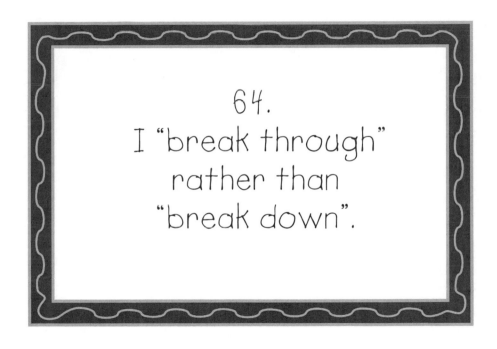

64.
I "break through"
rather than
"break down".

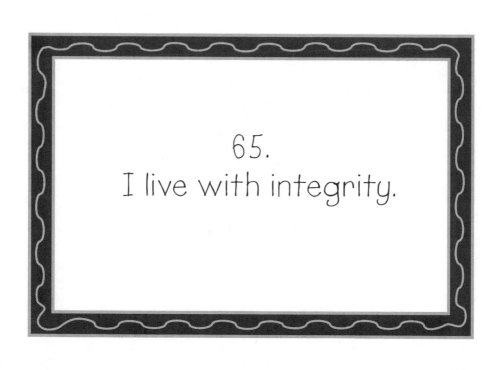

65.
I live with integrity.

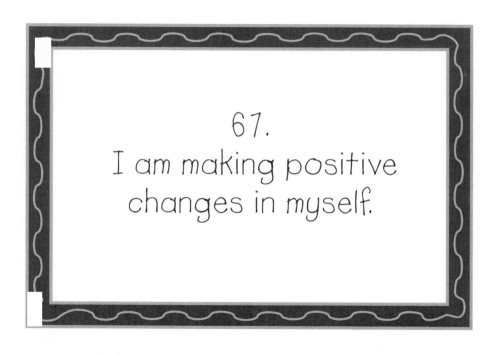

67.
I am making positive
changes in myself.

68.
My energy
energizes me.

69.
I am an
inspiration to myself.

70.
I am not afraid
to care.

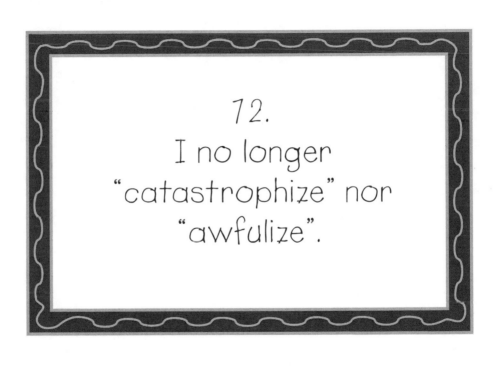

72.
I no longer
"catastrophize" nor
"awfulize".

73.
I accept
the weather.

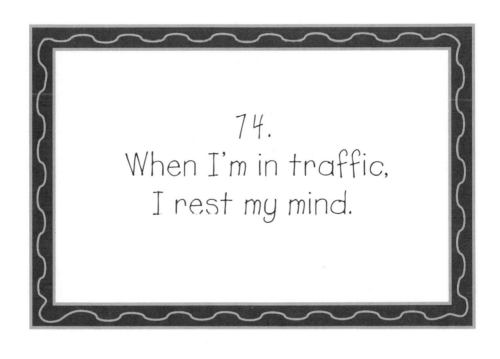

74.
When I'm in traffic,
I rest my mind.

75.
When things get tough,
I hum.

76.
My home is
my sanctuary.

77.
I am judging others
less often.

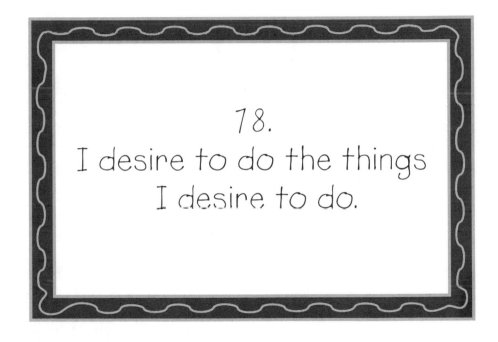

78.
I desire to do the things
I desire to do.

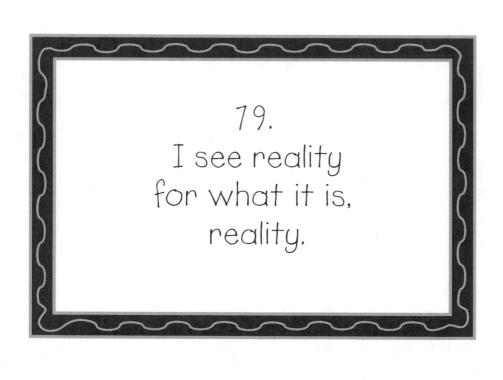

79.
I see reality
for what it is,
reality.

80.
I control my car,
not other people.

81.
I am no longer
my anger.

83.
When things change,
I change.

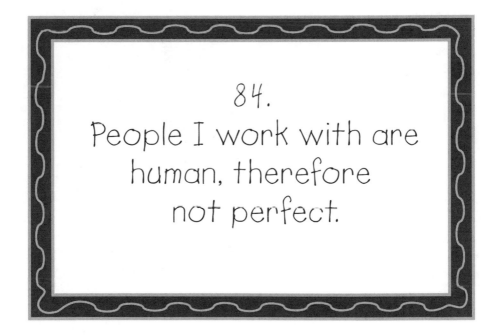

84.
People I work with are
human, therefore
not perfect.

85.
I strive for excellence,
not perfection.

86.
I expand
my mind daily.

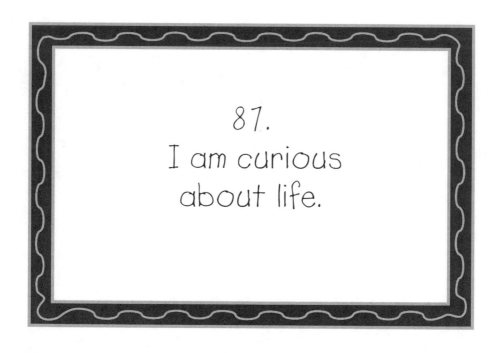

87.
I am curious
about life.

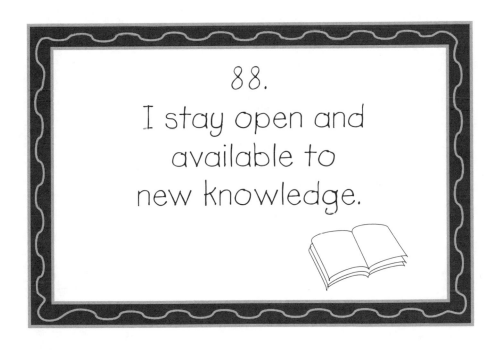

88.
I stay open and
available to
new knowledge.

89.
My income now exceeds my expenses.

90.
I think,
then I speak.

91.

The baggage of the past has become an overnight case.

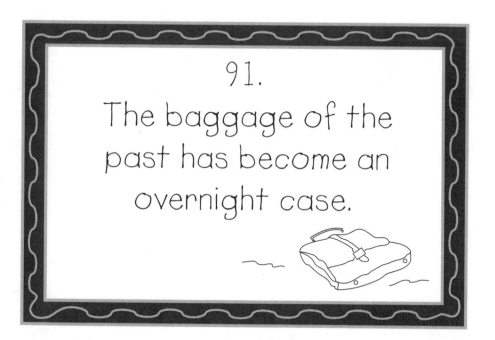

92.
I love
common sense.

93.
I am fun.

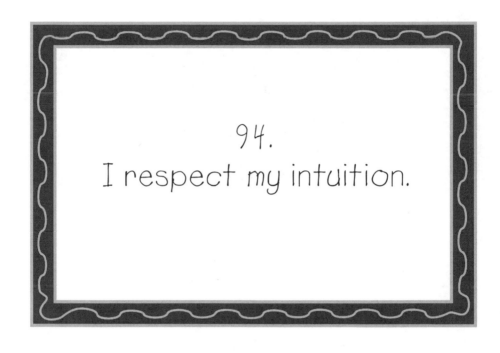

94.
I respect my intuition.

97.
I live with
grace and dignity.

98.
I "TADAH" each day.
Tomorrow is too late!

99.
I live a simple life.

100.
I am in harmony
with the universe.

101.
I enjoy silence.

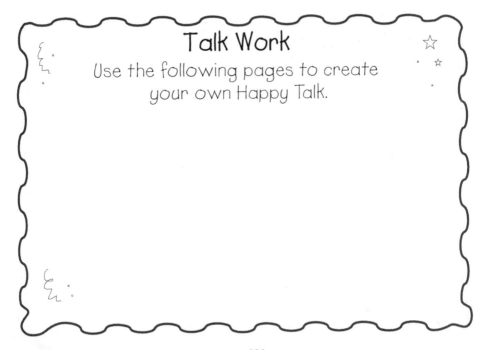

Talk Work

Use the following pages to create
your own Happy Talk.

keep going...

you're doing great!...

Wow!...

Loretta LaRoche is an educator, humorist and motivational speaker. She lectures nationally and internationally on various topics including:

"How to Prevent Hardening of the Attitude"
(Managing Stress Through Humor and Choice)
"Love, Laughter and Lasagna"
"Surviving Change Through Wit and Wisdom"
" Whine, Women and Song"
and **"Parenting with Humor".**

For Information on Loretta's Seminars and catalog call:
1-800-998-2324
E-Mail: stressed@tiac.com

page 135